While I Was Sleeping

Sheila Aldous

CloseToTheEdge Books

First published by
CloseToTheEdge Books, Devon, in 2021.
closetotheedgebooks@gmail.com

ISBN 978-1-3999-0625-8

Printed and bound by Imprint Digital, Devon.
www.digital.imprint.co.uk

Although inspired by real events, this work is fiction, and does not intend an exact portrayal of any event or person, living or dead.

For all my cousins

Acknowledgments

Special thanks to Edward Aldous for his constant support, proof-reading, his desk-top publishing skills, and his commitment to work late into the night; also to my family for their encouragement.

Contents

Preface

This poetry collection is based on the story of a Catholic mother, seriously ill in hospital. While she is semi-conscious, a priest forces her to renounce her daughter, who is then adopted. Despite searching for the rest of her life, the mother never sees her daughter again. These poems bring into focus the mother's vulnerability, her hospitalisation, and her despair at the forced removal of her daughter. Too late, and after her mother's death, the daughter eventually finds her birth family.

On 23rd September 2021 the Joint Committee on Human Rights began looking into forced adoptions and the role played by legal consent of the parents in any adoption, and how consent was given. The chairman, Harriet Harman QC MP, said "Everyone has the right to family life."

While I Was Sleeping

Can You Hear Me

can you hear me calling
as I fall through
      deep
         dark
            space

i am awake
    sleeping

are you waiting like me
in this nature world
where Orpheus wants
to take me down
rob us of each other
take me to a place
where we cannot find
      our
        twin
          souls

i will cling to a vine
climb up again to you
      not
        falling
         falling
like this through clouds

The Offering

We will pay well, Father.
A new roof is it?
A holiday for the Fathers?

Our gratitude
our beatitude
our blessing
our miracle.

We are a childless couple,
good Catholics, Father,
a good home, Father.
We will pay well, Father.

That one, that child at Mass, Father,
the one who genuflects so prettily
the one with the red-gold hair.

The Father considered,
asked the Mother, the one set
in the glass-stained window
bordered in black,
considered the stain of sin:
the money.

He would see to the paperwork,
make the arrangements.

Stained Glass

Hospital gowns glide forward, back,
an orchestra of scalpels clatter,
disinfected air gags, carbolic sucks up
the stench of maternal sin.

A moan is lost in space, flying away,
morphine-injected stars glow.
A mouth blue at the edges tries to speak.
Nuns hover, angels lip-syncing in a silent movie.

A circle of white rings a throat.
     Holy Holy Holy
It sprinkles her, water lands on her face,
wine splashes her lips. A crucifix swings over her:
she kisses the wounds on the cross.

She asks for her child, calls her name
over and over again. The priest turns away.
She has signed away the fruit of her womb.
     It won't be long now.

* * * * * * * *

A kaleidoscope bursts, sun pours through
fragments, blood red, magenta for penitence,
the green of paradise, the gold of her child's hair.
Black borders keep her in.

4

Stolen in the Name of Christ

There it is: the nature
of the wind, renouncing
the gift of light, carrying
in its mouth a brutal storm.

Oaks wrenched from root,
hedgerows loosened from red
cliffs of crumbling sand,
and bone and flesh ripped apart.
The mother gives in to sleep.

A white vestment cloaks
the theft, and banks the deed.
All nature has shifted
in a blink, while fever
burned in a tormented night.

Morning finds
a frozen heart,
a rosary ring,
a Mass said,
a tree stripped bare.

While I was Sleeping

When they told me you had gone
that I had signed you away
in between slipping through a dark tunnel
and seeing the light
I did not believe them.

There were spaces
where voices burbled in quiet murmurs
where snakes coiled around my bed
where a dark figure spoke
through a black haze of medication,
so quiet
his holy voice lulled me with a caress.

I try to grasp from that ether
what it was he was saying
over and over.
Better off, she'll be better off
she'll be better off.
Sign here, here, sign here.

When I wake my mind
is an ice-cold tundra
where nothing lives on this harsh plain –
forced away.

Remembrance

Little did I know when I named you
you'd be just a fleeting glance.

I did not see your milk teeth wiggle,
your new teeth take their place.

I did not get to teach you to read,
to wave you off for your first day at school.

We did not have a last hug. You squeezed me
as if you wanted to hold on to me forever.

I didn't get to know the things a mother should:
measles, chicken pox, mumps, scarlet fever,
be there to wipe your brow, hold your hand.

I thought I saw you. Once I saw a shadow
in the house at an upstairs window.

Was that you – rosemary for consecration,
peace of mind, purification,
protection, for a blessing,
for remembrance?

Returning Tide

Carried on golden wings
I shook off deathly seas,
grasped the holy water of life:
imagined you back in my arms.

Nurses scuttled like frightened mice,
witnesses – aware of the theft.
The priest ceased his visits, hid
in some corner of his ancient church.

Maybe he was washing his vestments.
Maybe he was on his knees asking for pardon.
Maybe he was running from his own sin.
Maybe from his secret greed.

Maybe praying for absolution.
This barterer of my child,
selling to the highest bidder
and pulling up the anchor from its mooring
setting her adrift, far from me.

From the safety of my beach I watch the sea-mist roll in,
wait for a patch of blue to open up, to shine through.

Seabirds toss and lift, rise and fly free,
wheel with joy, swoop in pleasure
round and round, wings outstretched,
round and round and back.

.

Snowman

He had come round for tea, and mother
set up the cardboard hoop-la on the door.
It swung impossibly out of target every
time my spying sister barged through.
He and I played on, not yet adults,
until mother asked us to post a letter.

The ground, soft with baby crystals, was clean
underneath our feet, and we walked on
through a pure citadel of trees. Moonlight
winked through white coated branches,
and I watched him become clothed
in snow until his collar was full and cold.

Our breath swirled in the remnants of innocence,
flowering liquid glass on the shining panes of night.

Our feet trod carefully crossing
to the other side under the heavy fall.
We had no clues or markers except for our
footsteps, small craters making the path
to show us what was next.

The red postbox disguised its knowing face,
opened a yawning mouth to receive
the envelope, as we gave in to that first kiss.
In that glittery moment away from the cardboard
cut-outs, we had reached a summit, snowblinded
in the blizzard, spinning our own snowglobe.

Marram Grass

Side-by-side our backs to the sun
I listen to thunder pounding
and it is my heart in the clamour
hanging on his every word.

Did you know, he said, *from this we could
weave our home, hold back the storm?*

He waved his arms wide
showed me the world
until a canopy of light
studded the dark, until stars
and black sea were one.

That night I lay under his promise.
We reached out for each other again,
sheltered in the bank of marram.

Crossing the Line

The quick fumble was a mistake.
I vomited up the salt-stale
sting of fag smoke. Drenched
myself in the drowning-land
of a steam-hot shower.
I should have waited
the customary twelve months,
at least worn the widow's weeds.
But I had needed it now –
the sweet hum of summer.

Empty Shell

Afterwards the hush of breath,
a whisper in my ear,
the tide recedes
leaves me this shell:

this curve of body cracked
but still intact on shaken
foundations, built on
motherhood's stony ground.

I was in that other place
struggling in sand:
the last remnants
of my house split apart.

I had waded in too deep,
believed the promises
of happy-ever-afters
now drowned by falling rain.

Yellow Dress

It was late, the dress shop was closing.
I had to make a decision: the pink one
or the yellow, the colour of sunshine? The last time
I bought a yellow dress was for my child,
the last time the sun had come out.
Since then treading on dandelions or buttercups
sends a chill shooting down my spine.
The yellow one suits you best, a voice faded into
the darkening room. Mannequins emerged from every
corner, held up their hands in mock blessing.

Give me a few moments to decide, I am just thinking.
Thinking. But wires from my arms were holding me
back, stopping me dancing in the dark. Snake eyes blinked.

Yellow is the colour of my true love's hair ...
a tune was playing in my head. No, it had not
been yellow, it had been red gold, spun like
copper. This dark was circling around me, taking
me by the throat. The mannequins were holding
pens, paper, syringes. The wires were tying me up,
thick ropes keeping me down, hissing hysterically.
I had to get away, run, take my child and run.
The assistant interrupts. *Well?*
I'll take it, I say, *the yellow one.*

Counting Blossoms

The apple tree outside
my world is full of blossom,
my window is full of blossom.
It is a good year for blossom.

I count the years
the silent years.
I count the blossoms
and they are the days
since you were taken.
I try to remember
your face, what you
might look like now.

The days fall away
litter the ground:
I see you, I see you.

Into the Light

I creak with breath of bone,
of too many cruel winds, days
of blow-by-blows that shut out
your light.

I say: *Don't you worry.*
Do not think of dark days, think
of horses lifting up their well-shod
hooves, whisking into a froth,
seas white and crested, bringing
you back to me.

I call to you from folds of fire:
Sing pretty one, breathe fresh
clean air, leave the assault,
learn to dance to your future.

Silver Bullets

I walk the same ground you walk,
we are leaves blowing in the wind.

Did they lie – say you were unwanted?
Did they tell you I abandoned you?

The fallen moon hides its face in thick cloud,
knows what it has done. I am bone-broken,
flesh-forlorn, limb-languished, lip-split.

What is there left but to stand here,
watch for the shadow in the house?

Will you look out of the nursery window,
see the torch I burn for you, remember
the poppies – your father's courage?

His trust in me to keep you safe?
I am in confession, without grace. I crawl
on my knees. The night is heavy as stone.

Rain falls on the streets. I am shrouded
in withered laurels – shut out.

You are behind enemy doors: renunciated.
I am alive but mortally wounded. Silver bullets
of wine and bread fell me: I bleed.

Kissing in the Dark

I cannot sleep again: 3am
and my feet are in and out,
kicking off the covers, tossing,
turning, thinking of her.
Sheets off, up to my chin,
left side, right side, back to front.

We had been dancing a do-si-do,
laughing back to back, two ballerinas
pirouetting around each other,
not quite touching.

Where are you, are you
on this side of the planet?
Have you moved
to another continent?

Are you just doorsteps away,
a woman all grown up?
Are you weighing heartbeats too,
measuring this maternal visit?
Are you kissing me in the dark?

Would I know you if we ran
for the same bus, would we fight
for a parking space? Or say
No, you go, you go before me,
you have more to carry than me.

Moments in the Lichen Field

Last night I was given
a gift of butterflies.
I flew with them over
fields where lichen dressed
the arms of trees.
I looked above puffed-up clouds
saw the rebirth of a new world
suckled on sweetwater.

The lake filled with turquoise pools.
A dragonfly illuminated my reflection
Soft pebbles soothed my feet
pulled me back to green fields
where oxygen restored my balance,
guided me with a map
of firm earth-bound ground.

In the Shamble of the Rain

In blue skies we were in murmuration,
a babble colouring the world,
until our namby-pamby words
disappeared into a quietude of petals –
until the silence
separated us
cut apart our shadows.

This day blossoms fall
on empty hollows.
Our naked bones, soured fruits,
huddle together in memory.
Tongue-tied we wait until our story
writes itself, speaks
the vanished truth –
for that is all we have
in the shamble of the rain.

Snowberries

You are, in your way, my Winter's Tale:
you glisten like snowberries who lie in wait.
Wilding ghosts, scant of skin, thread gossip,
hand me a tray of frenzied omens filled

with scaremongering. Your suitcase rests,
stuffed with ivory shrouds you will forever wear
on a journey that started out so well:
free from gossip of a Spring-death.

I reach up and find a spider in my hair
knitting me a trap on your threshold.
It slips in a smile from your hiding place,
so I will always know the very thing I've lost.

A Prayer to the Shepherd

Am I the sinner they say I am? Where is the rescue you promised? You did not rid me of the dangerous animals. You allowed a dangerous animal to fool me, to masquerade as a friend. He came with wine and a promise, with music and love songs. He lulled me to sleep on a steep hill high above the earth, and my soul was stolen. My sin was to believe. Tell me where she is, where I can find her, only then can I leave this valley of dry bones. Bring me back from this dark place. On that disastrous day, I was hungry, yet no one fed me, I was thirsty, yet my thirst has not been slaked. I am lost, so heal me, return my scattered lamb, show me the tree bearing fruit, a time for mending. Give me back my child.

Too Late

The television station had run the strap.
Small nuggets to tempt a bored public
in the ad-breaks, until programme producers
got bored too, and edited out
the mother's name.

Maternal instinct had clung on.
Her prayers went unheard
mumbled from her desert throat,
her last kiss on the rosary
slipping from her grasp.
She carried her child within
the secret of her rib-bone
through a dark valley
into an eddy of dust.

Forever

I would never forget my mother's smile
although they said I had to.
She was like Greta Garbo,
a mystery woman who floated
out of my life one confusing day.

Today I am filling the kitchen with light,
courtesy of an orchestra of bees
reminding me that there is still
honey in the hive.

Later I walk past the perfume counter
of the High Street department store.
I sense she is with me, at my shoulder
picking me up, twirling me round,
round until my giggles fill the wind.
She surrounds me
with the scent of honeyed oil,
wild-flower meadows, lavender, rosemary.

Return of Nature

I came back to her that day.
The first blossom
was not the last blossom.

The flickering fires of October
were doused and gone.

I saw differently the ghost,
the absence of her touch,
saw the colours merge
from grey to gold.

I came back to her that day.
The last blossom
was the first blossom.

The flickering flames, if I look
closely, were simply resting.

Voices of Testimony

A magpie hopped in front of the car:
he wore a black armband
and carried a gold-topped cane.
His top hat ruffled his feathers
and he led a procession of six more
dancing behind the iron park gate.

The bones of them jittered when
they rattled and rolled, and I knew then
I was late on my way to that cul-de-sac home.
Waiting to process was the leading man,
who had contacts and keys to the big house
in the clouds, in the marbled city of Rome.

The front door swung open, the witnesses
foretold, embroidered in rich texture
the deathly scene, and there she was
reclining, as if a queen, awash
with incense, the rising, the blue.

Inspired by The Death of the Virgin,
Pieter Bruegel the Elder, c. 1564.

Sometimes it is Good to be in the Rain

I tap in the post code, take the road
away from the tunnel of rain.
The bruises of yesterday's sky
have cleared. I travel through
the golden halo around Haytor,
smile in the slash of morning.

I brave a flood to get here.
The Canonteign Falls – a woman's
tears – twinned with mine –
where I think no end to sorrow is in sight.

But then I see she is that nymph
that other of me. She takes me
by the hand, holds my head
in cupped palms, pours redeeming water,
immerses me in her myth.

The further from home I drive
the better the weather.
I wind down the window,
punch the air, gulp in
a measured cup of ozone.

This is how it should always be: breathing
as though I've never breathed before.
My lungs invite earthy scents,
the promise of flower-dressed fields,
of heather, of moors,
of sunlit rain and shadow.

I lift my face to this cloudless sky, marvelling
as though I have never marvelled before,
watch a rim of light
pillow the horizon.
And I am thankful to whoever it is
for showing me the way.

Remembrance Avenue

Guilty! The month of October
robbing the trees of leaves.
It was nothing to do with the way
you danced, or with the oaks
as they leaned into each other
in a slow waltz.

Nor how my shoulders ached
on the way to church,
my arms heavy with the weight
of keeping her close again,
our limbs a last time as one.
I did not mind her halting the cars
on Remembrance Avenue.
Or the mourners who did not know her
who made the sign of the cross.
I did not mind the doves
released to point her to a crying sky.
I did not mind
                    until her face
turned away from the sun.

The Art of Flying

I don't see her as ash.
By now, she will have perfected the art of flying:
she will be a competitor of high stakes,
      taking a bet to beat the odds.

      Like some talent show contestant
in a jungle, my mother will take on the challenge
resurface without the benefit of experience,
      blink in the new sunlight.

I know she was not without sin, but her
redemption is attempting to turn over
under heaving stone, until she kicks sudden
death back to life. I'd vote for her to win.

      By now she'll be divested of sinew,
will polish her bones bit-by-bit with
the iron of earth, be a winner, glowing
      in the pit where she now lives.

I try not to dwell on the maudlin, or recreate
a picture in my mind of her crumbling away,
at the mercy of a Shylock, calling in the debt,
taking off her flesh like a dress.

      If I was a gambler, I'd bet on her,
not as ash. I would see her, sliding through
the interstices between my space and hers,
      fully clothed and coming up for air.